MY FIRST BOOK OF
TODDLER
ACTIVITIES

Woo! Jr. Kids Activities Founder: Wendy Piersall

Book Layout by: Lilia Garvin
Cover Illustration: Michael Koch

Published by DragonFruit, an imprint of Mango Publishing, a division of Mango Media Inc.

For permission requests, please contact the publisher at:

Mango Publishing Group
2850 Douglas Road, 2nd Floor
Coral Gables, FL
33134 USA
info@mango.bz

For special orders, quantity sales, course adoptions and corporate sales, please email the publisher at sales@mango.bz. For trade and wholesale sales, please contact Ingram Publisher Services at customer.service@ingramcontent.com or +1.800.509.4887.

My First Book of Toddler Activities: Letters, Shapes, Colors, Numbers, and More Educational Activities for Toddlers

ISBN: (p) 978-1-64250-711-9
BISAC: JNF001010 JUVENILE NONFICTION / Activity Books / Coloring

My First Toddler Activity Book

Welcome to this big book of toddler activities! It includes everything you need: tracing, matching, color recognition, pattern recognition, coloring, and much, much more!

Follow the instructions on each page, and have fun! Grab your favorite crayons, pencils, or markers, and let's go!

Find the Matching Pair

Practice tracing on this maple leaf!

maple leaf

One

There is one rose.

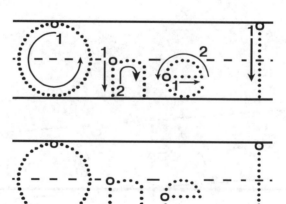

Find the one ladybug!

TWO

There are two apples.

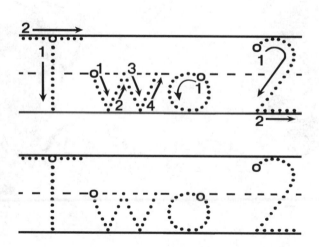

Which two bunnies match?

Three

There are three beehives.

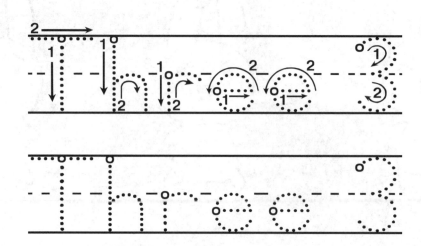

There are three dinosaurs. Circle the number three!

1   2   3

Four

There are four baby elephants.

Help the Bee get to the Biggest of the four Beehives!

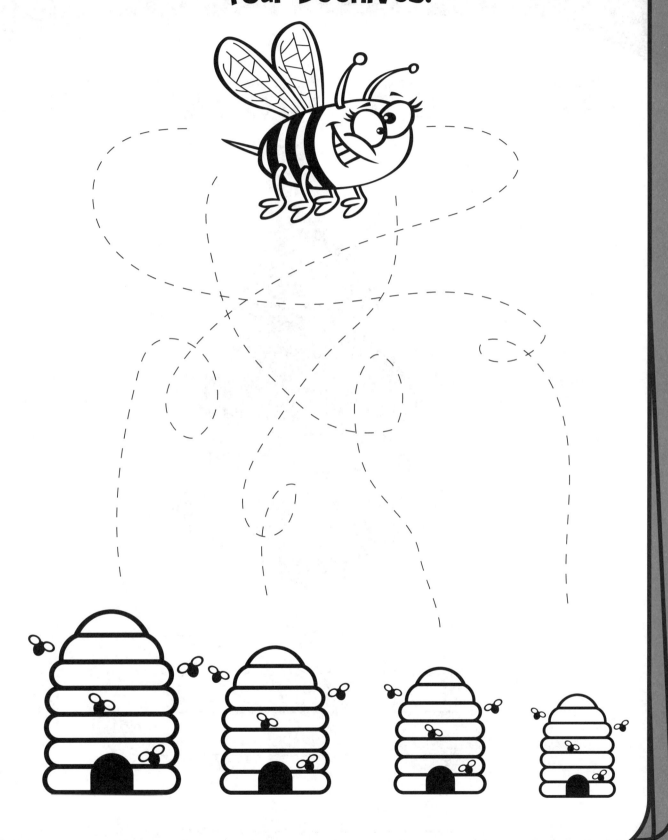

Five

There are five buttons.

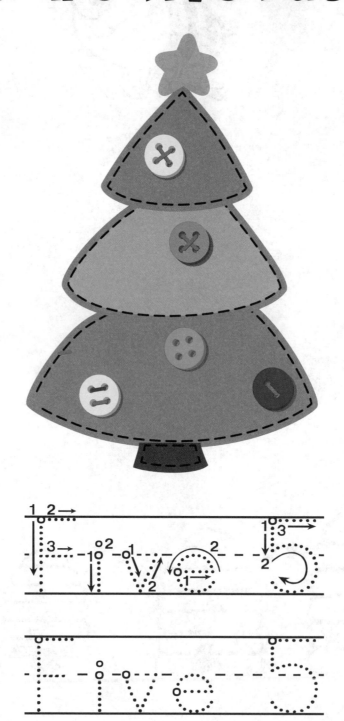

Match the five shadows!

Six

There are six foxes.

Trace the line to match the six flowers, then color them!

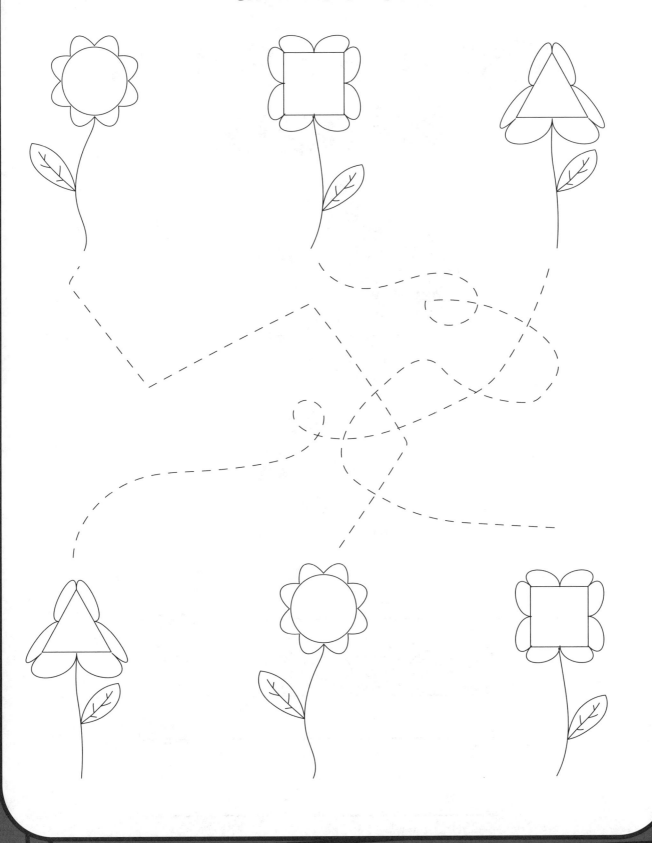

Seven

There are seven balloons.

Trace & color the seven spots on the turtle's shell!

Eight

There are eight birds.

Trace & color the eight trash bags!

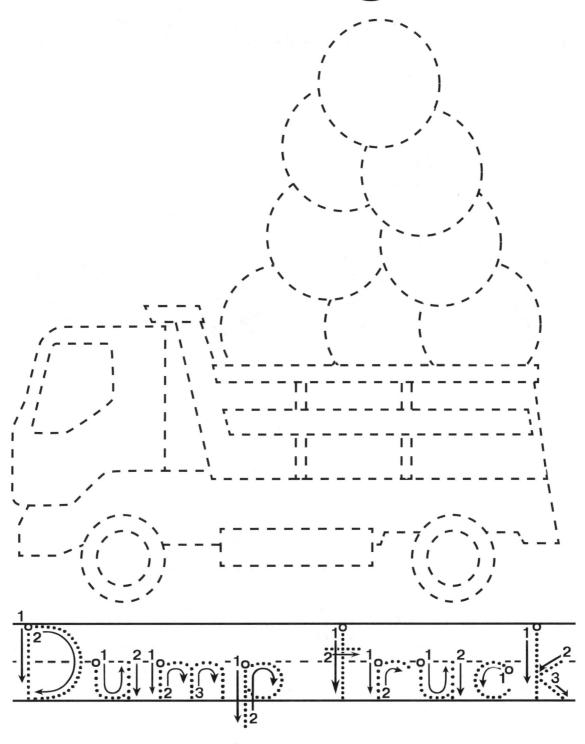

Nine

There are nine flowers.

These aliens have nine eyes.
Help them get to their friends!

Ten

There are ten raindrops.

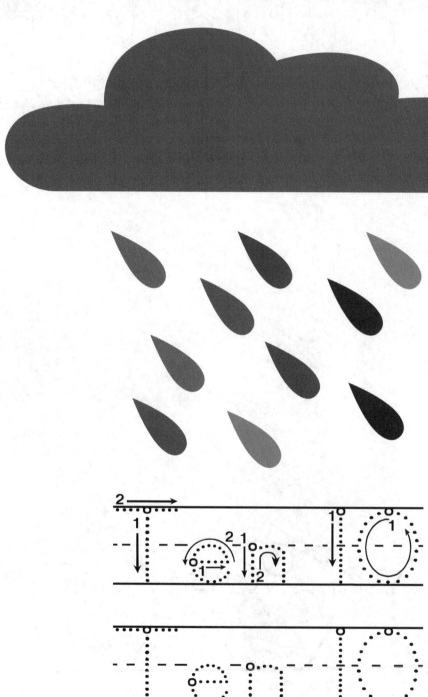

Finish the ten dots!

Blue

Color me!

Green

Color me!

Find & color the Hidden Pictures!

Red

color me!

Purple

Color me!

Finish the Dot to Dot!

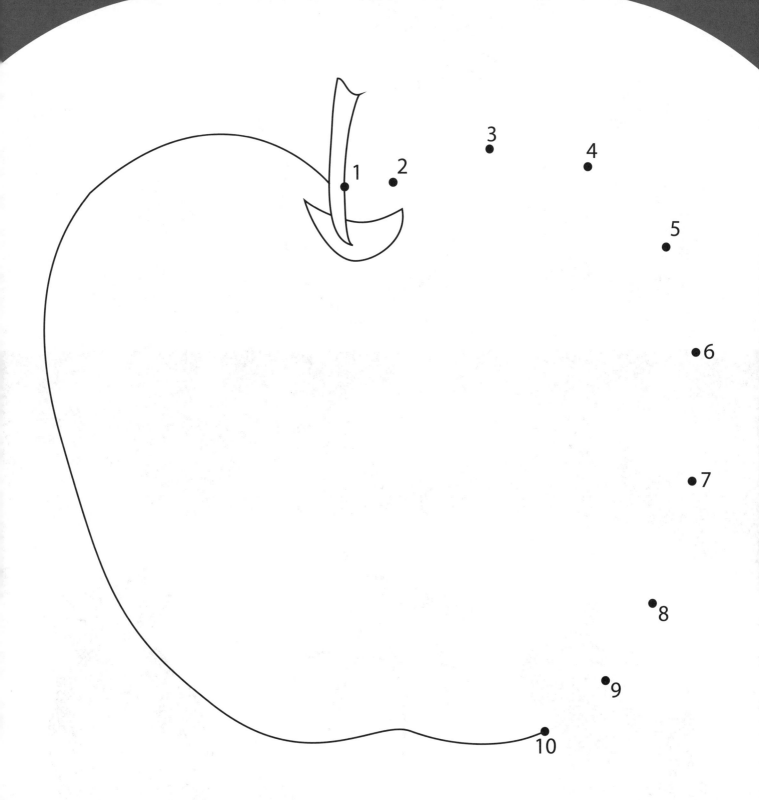

Yellow

Color me!

Orange

Color me!

Match the Parents & Babies!

Black

color me!

Brown

color me!

Trace & color

color Matching!

■ Red

■ Black

■ Blue

■ Yellow

■ Brown

Trace the line that leads the hen to her nest!

Find & color the Hidden Pictures!

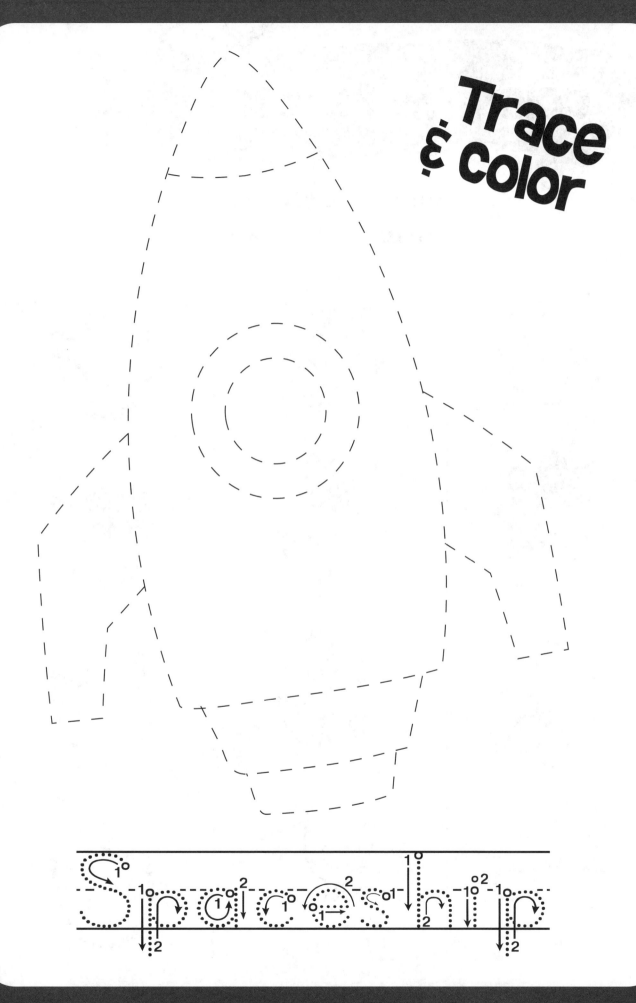

Trace & color

Spaceship

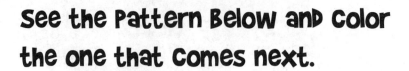

Color The Pattern

See the pattern below and color the one that comes next.

Yellow

Yellow Yellow

Color the things that are yellow.

Trace & color

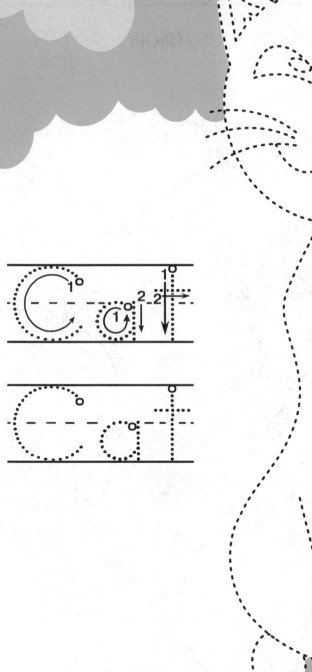

Crown Delivery Tracing

Help the kawaii crown be delivered to the pink Queen cat!

Color me!

How many Raindrops?

circle the number of raindrops:

3   5   7   6   4

1   9   4   3   2

7   8   2   4   9

5   8   4   2   6

3   1   6   4   2

Finish the Dot to Dot!

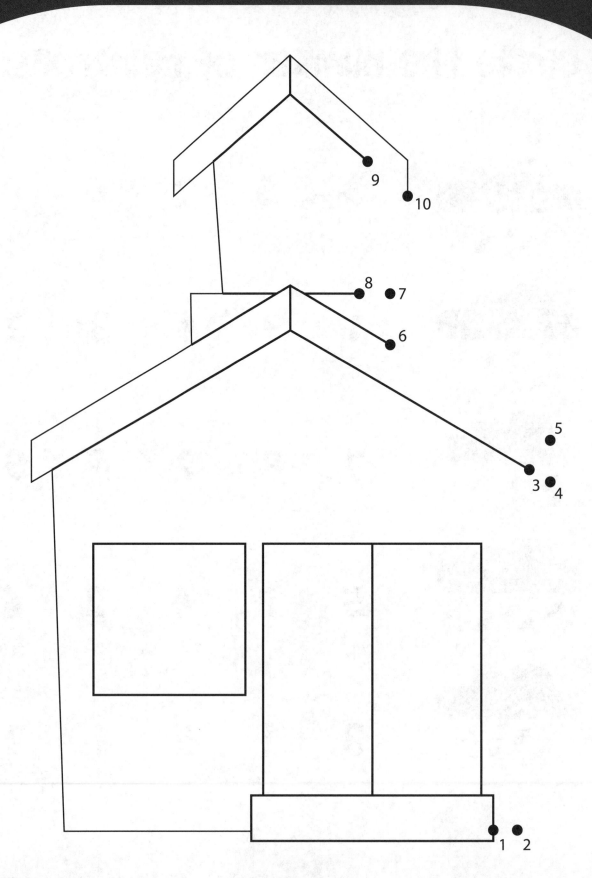

Trace & color

maple leaf

maple leaf

Color me Red!

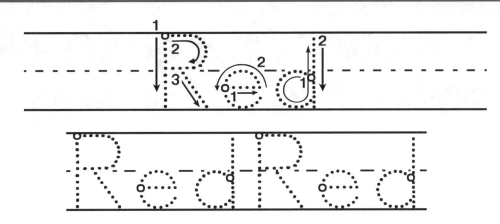

Color the things that are red.

Use the color Orange to guide the ambulance to the hospital!

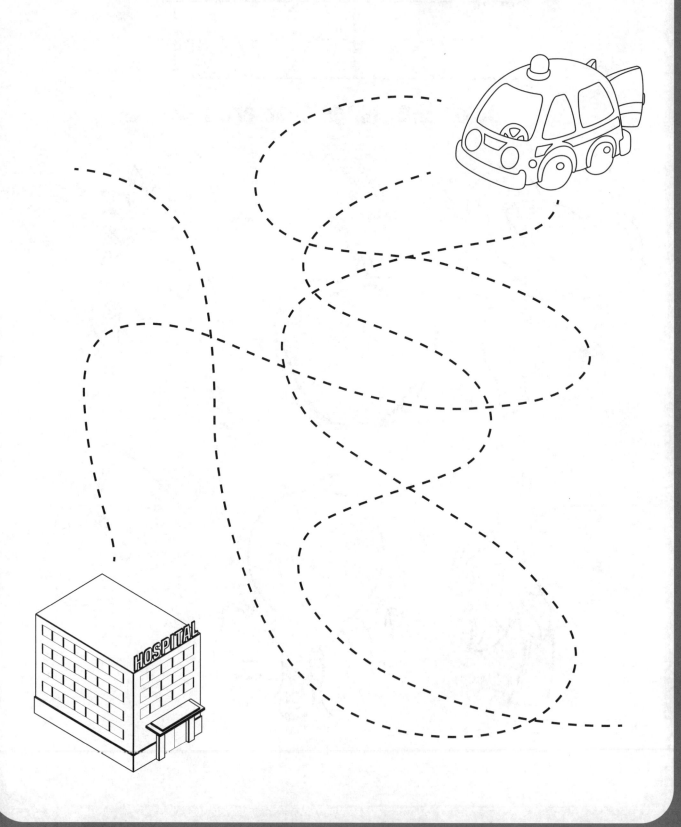

Trace & color me Orange & Red

Comet

Trace & color me Green

Dinosaur

Match the Baby Dinosaurs to their Parents!

Color the whale blue!

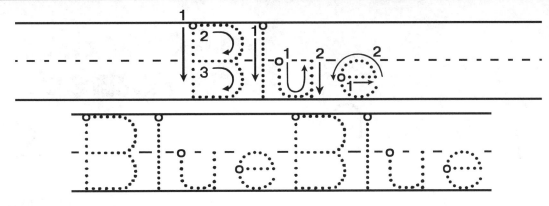

Blue

Color the things that are Blue.

Find & color the Hidden Pictures!

Match the Leaves!

color the square with the matching leaf green:

Match the missing pieces!

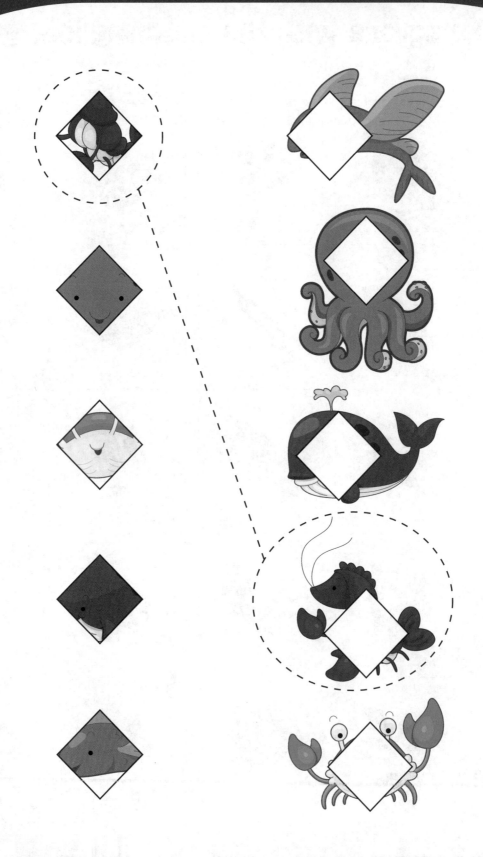

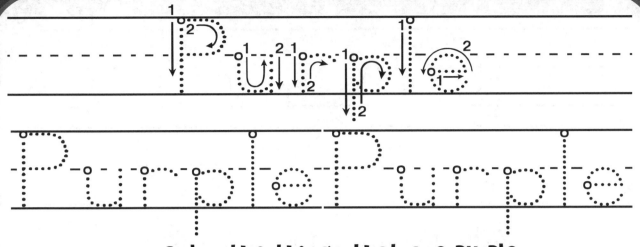

Purple Purple

Color the things that are PURPLE.

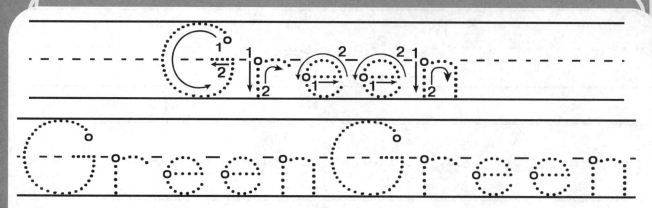

Green

GreenGreen

color the things that are green.

Match the Reptile Shadows!

color the frogs and lily pads, then trace the lines!

Color me Blue!

Find & color the Hidden Pictures!

Match the Dinosaurs

Match the two remaining Pairs of Dinosaurs!

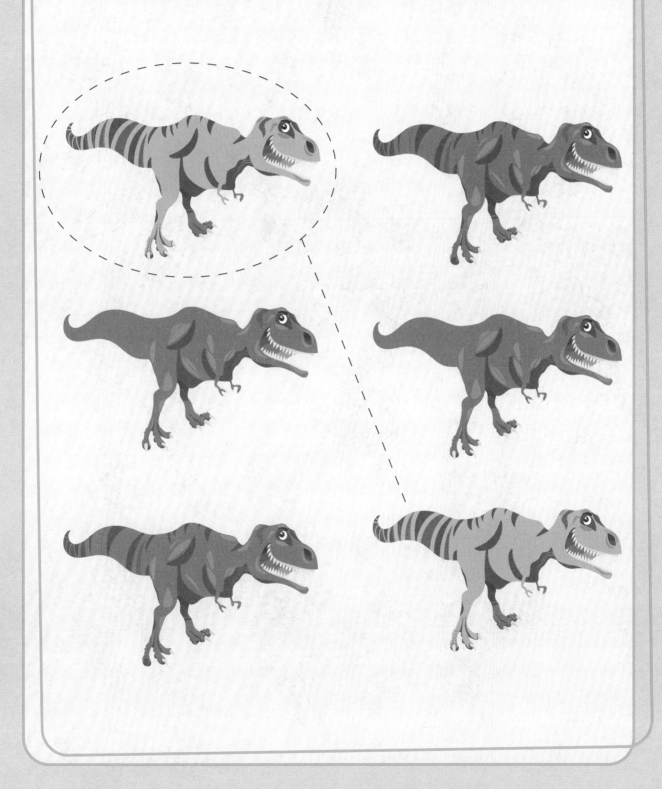

Trace and color the squares blue, the triangles yellow, and the circles red!

Trace & Color

Color me!

Match the Parents & Babies!

Spot 5 Differences!

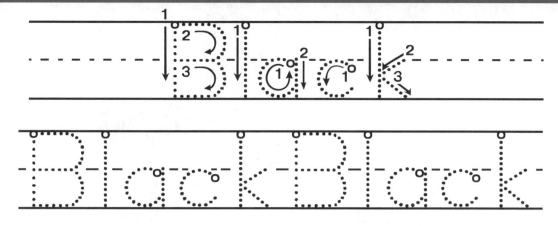

Color the things that are Black.

Spot 5 Differences!

Trace and Color the North Pole!

Welcome to the North Pole!

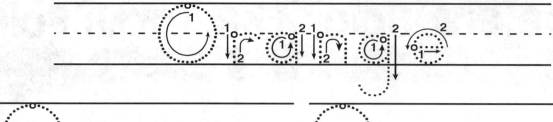

Orange Orange

Color the things that are orange.

Finish the Dot to Dot!

Find & color the Hidden Pictures!

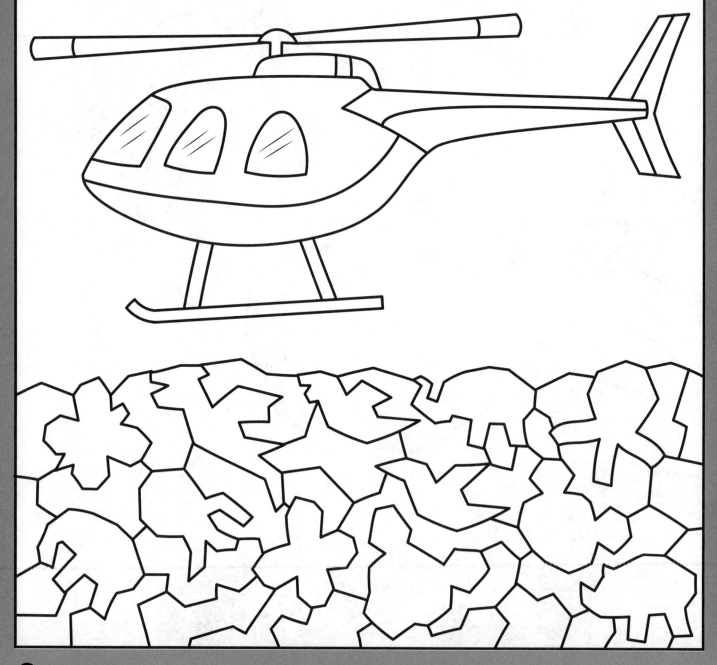

Guide the Helicopters to their landing pads!

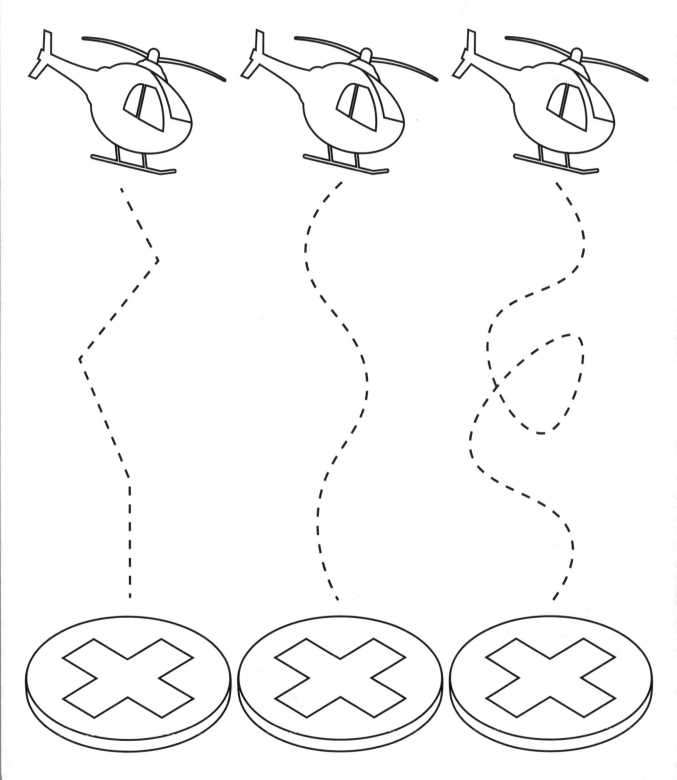

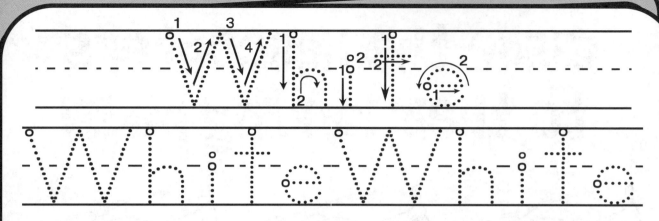

Color or circle the things that are white.

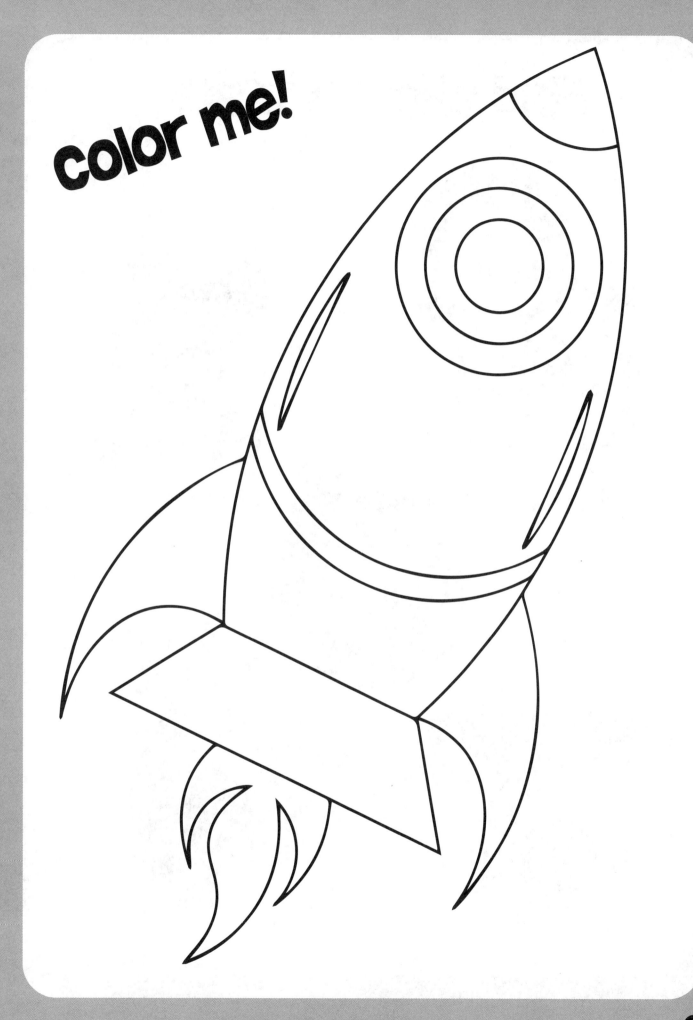

Color me!

Find the Dinosaur

Color Matching!

■ **Blue**

■ **Yellow**

■ **Purple**

■ **Green**

■ **Red**

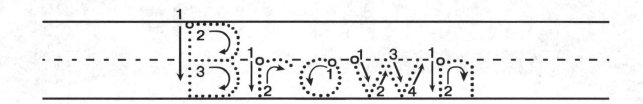

Brown

Color the things that are Brown.

Spot 3 Differences!

Find & color the Hidden Pictures!

Finish the Dot to Dot!

Find the Elephant

Trace & Color

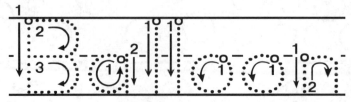

Finish the Dot to Dot!

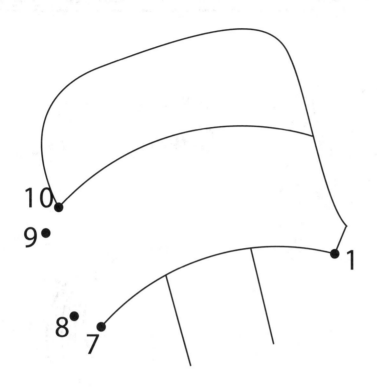

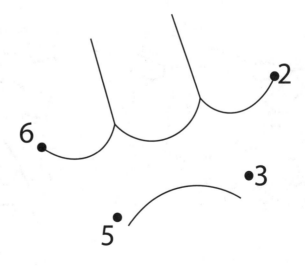

Find & color the Hidden Pictures!

Trace & color

What color are these?

Color the bee yellow!

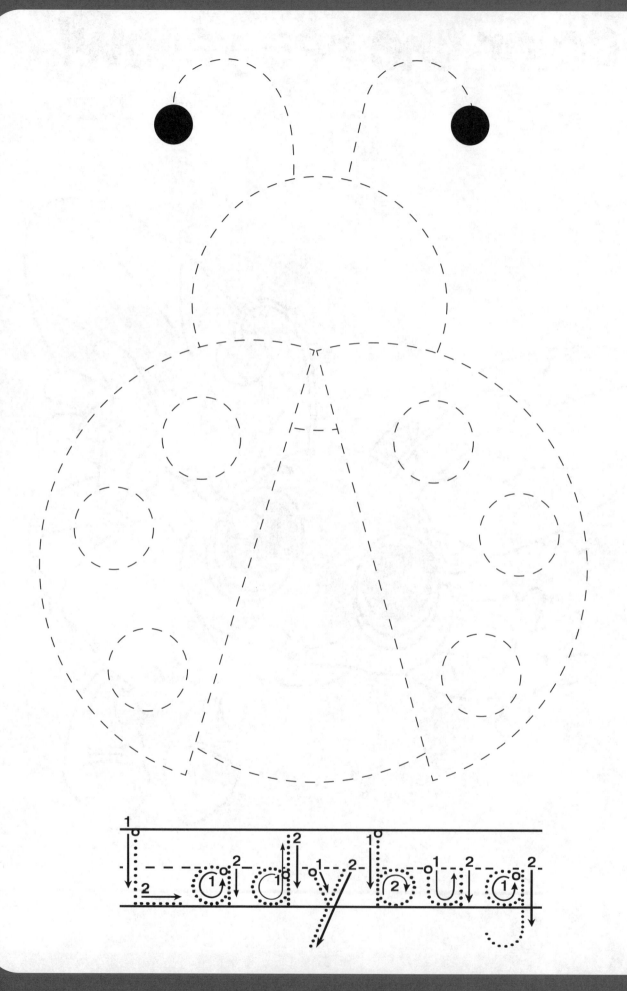

Find the Ladybug

Trace & color

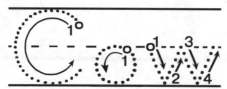

Find & color the Hidden Pictures!

Trace & color

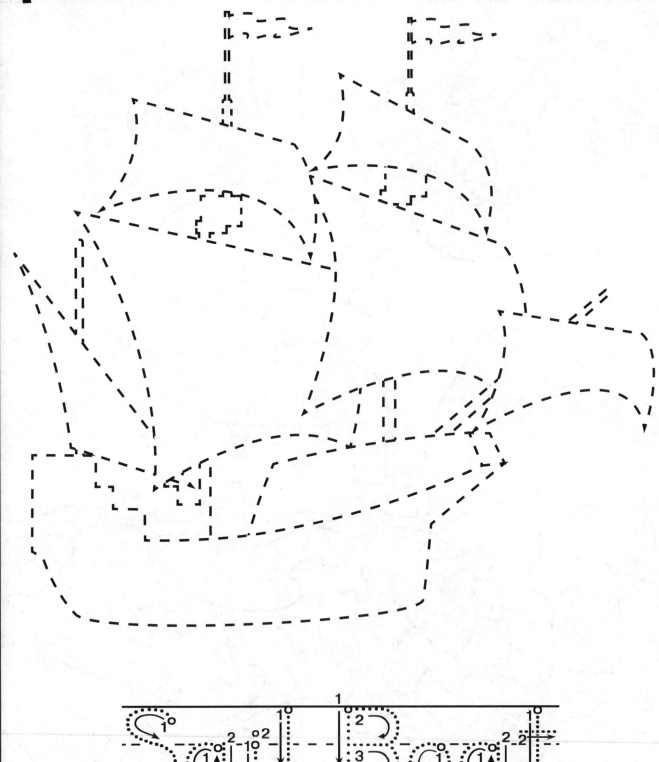

Sail Boat

Color the anchor black!

What color are these?

Find the Blue Bird

Gingerbread
Man

Spot 3 Differences!

Find & color the Hidden Pictures!

Trace & color

Cupcake

Find the Beetle

Find & color the Hidden Pictures!

Trace
& color

Honey Bee

color me!

Match the Missing pieces!

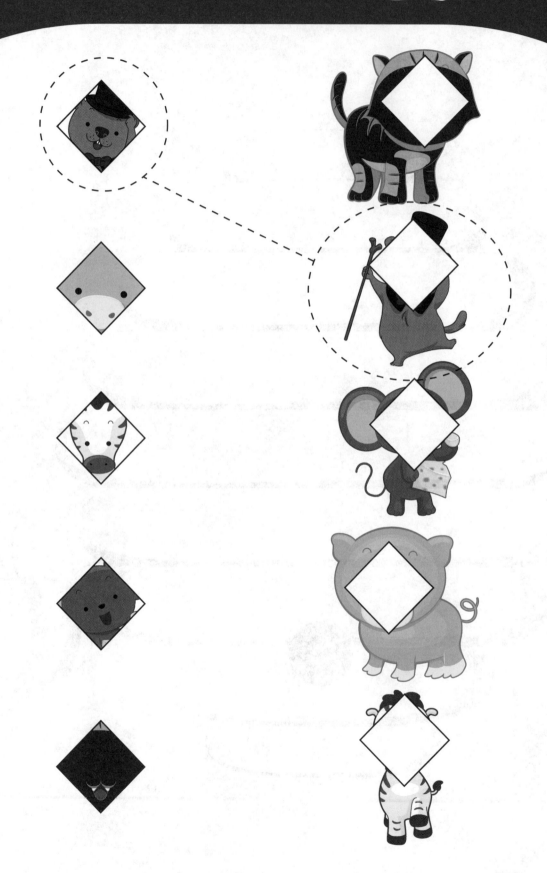

Find & color the Hidden Pictures!

DragonFruit, an imprint of Mango Publishing, publishes high-quality children's books to inspire a love of lifelong learning in readers. DragonFruit publishes a variety of titles for kids, including children's picture books, nonfiction series, toddler activity books, pre-K activity books, science and education titles, and ABC books. Beautiful and engaging, our books celebrate diversity, spark curiosity, and capture the imaginations of parents and children alike.

Mango Publishing, established in 2014, publishes an eclectic list of books by diverse authors. We were named the Fastest-Growing Independent Publisher by Publishers Weekly in 2019 and 2020. Our success is bolstered by our main goal, which is to publish high-quality books that will make a positive impact in people's lives.

Our readers are our most important resource; we value your input, suggestions, and ideas. We'd love to hear from you—after all, we are publishing books for you!

Please stay in touch with us and follow us at:

Instagram: @dragonfruitkids

Facebook: Mango Publishing

Twitter: @MangoPublishing

LinkedIn: Mango Publishing

Pinterest: Mango Publishing

Sign up for our newsletter at www.mangopublishinggroup.com and receive a free book! Join us on Mango's journey to change publishing, one book at a time.

Woo! Jr. Kids Activities is passionate about inspiring children to learn through imagination and FUN. That is why we have provided thousands of craft ideas, printables, and teacher resources to over 55 million people since 2008. We are on a mission to produce books that allow kids to build knowledge, express their talent, and grow into creative, compassionate human beings. Elementary education teachers, day care professionals, and parents have come to rely on Woo! Jr. for high-quality, engaging, and innovative content that children LOVE. Our bestselling kids activity books have sold over 300,000 copies worldwide.

     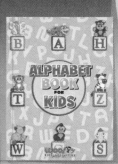

Tap into our free kids activity ideas at our website WooJr.com or by following us on social media:

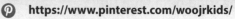